POWER PRESSURE COOKER XL COOKBOOK

The Essential Quick and Simple Pressure Cooker Cookbook for Weight Loss and Clean Eating

Table of Contents

INTRODUCTION

I want to thank you and congratulate you for getting a copy of the book, "Power Pressure Cooker XL Cookbook: The Essential Quick and Simple Pressure Cooker Cookbook For Weight Loss and Clean Eating".

This book contains proven steps and strategies on how to use the Power Pressure Cooker XL to come up with a variety of recipes. It features recipes that are healthy and easy to follow.

You don't need to deprive yourself in order to lose weight. You simply have to choose the right ingredients and eat moderately. You can use the recipes in this book as a guide in planning your meals.

Thanks again for getting a copy of this book, I hope you enjoy it!

CHAPTER 1

POWER PRESSURE COOKER XL BASICS

The Power Pressure Cooker XL is among the most in-demand pressure cookers in the market. It is efficient, easy to use, and budget-friendly. It comes in 6 Quart, 8 Quart, 8 Quart Deluxe and 10 Quart capacities.

It has the following one touch preset buttons:

- Delay Timer – Use this button to set the pressure cooker to begin cooking later in the day.

- Canning/Preserving – This setting cooks at 12 psi. You can actually opt to use this setting in pressure cooking any dish for 10 minutes and above. Use the Cook Time Selector to adjust the cooking duration to 45 and 120 minutes. The product's manual does not recommend pressure canning at an altitude higher than 12,000 feet.

- Time Adjustment – It allows you to manually adjust the cooking time after you have chosen a preset button. This is only used to add more cook time. Keep on pressing the button until you have reached the required cook time for your dish,

- Keep Warm/Cancel – You can cancel a function that you have selected or push the button to turn off the cooker. Every time the timer of the pressure cooker is up, it automatically goes to Keep Warm mode.

- Slow Cook – It has a preset 2-hour cook time. You can adjust it to 6 or 12 hours by pressing the Cook Time Selector.

Here are the other preset buttons that are typically used for pressure cooking. Choose the button with the closest cooking time to the recipe that you are doing. Take note that it doesn't have a minus button. This means that you cannot manually decrease cooking time. Choose the button with the closest time to what you are cooking and add more time as required. You can do this by pressing the Cook Time Selector button once or twice to choose from the available preset cook time or manually adjust the cook time by pressing the Time Adjustment button.

- Soup/Stew – Cook time is 10 minutes. Adjust to 30 minutes by pressing the Cook Time Selector button once or 60 minutes by pressing the same button twice.

- Rice/Risotto – Cook time is 6 minutes. Adjust to 18 minutes by pressing the Cook Time Selector button once or 25 minutes by pressing the same button twice.

- Beans/Lentils – Cook time is 5 minutes. Adjust to 15 minutes by pressing the Cook Time Selector button once or 30 minutes by pressing the same button twice.

- Fish/Vegetables Steam – Cook time is 2 minutes, which is the shortest setting in this cooker. Adjust to 4 minutes by pressing the Cook Time Selector button once or 10 minutes by pressing the same button twice.

- Chicken/Meat – Cook time is 15 minutes. Adjust to 40 minutes by pressing the Cook Time Selector button once or 60 minutes by pressing the same button twice.

This pressure cooker doesn't have a Saute/Browning button, but this brand has other models that have this feature. When using the cooker for this purpose, select any preset button. A good choice for sautéing your ingredients is the **CHICKEN/MEAT** button because it has the longest cook time among all the preset buttons. Make sure that the lid is off. Press the **CHICKEN/MEAT** button. Once the pot heats up, start sautéing/browning your ingredients.

When all the ingredients are inside the pot, put the lid on and set the valve to close/pressure mode. Press the Keep Warm/Cancel button to reset the timer. Select the preset button with the closest time setting to what you are cooking and adjust time by either pressing the Cook Time Selector button once or twice or the Time Adjustment button continuously until you have reached the required cook time setting.

The digital panel at this point will start spinning. This means that the cooker is gathering pressure. It will automatically begin counting the set cook time once the pressure is up. At this point, the lid will automatically lock as the pressure cooking process begins.

The Power Pressure Cooker XL cooks at 7.2 psi, except when used for pressure canning. It has two valves in the lid. Set it to pressure position to start cooking and put it into the steam position to release pressure when you are done.

This pressure cooker comes with an inner lid with a gasket and an outer lid. In cleaning the liner, use the pull tab to detach the gasket and liner from the lid. Take the gasket off the liner and clean it. Make sure that the pull tab is visible when you put the parts together.

The Power Pressure Cooker XL employs the flavor infusion technology. It traps heat inside the pot that forces moisture into your ingredients. This allows the preservation of the nutrients of all the ingredients and it also locks in the right flavor to your dishes.

The Power Pressure Cooker XL is easy and safe to use. The lid won't open while there is still pressure inside. This pressure cooker is a good value for its price. You can use it to come up with a variety of dishes – from soups, main dish, to snacks and desserts.

CHAPTER 2

POWER PRESSURE COOKER XL BREAKFAST RECIPES

Healthy Quinoa Breakfast

Prep time: 5 min
Cook time: 2 min
Servings: 6

Ingredients

- 1/4 teaspoon of ground cinnamon
- A pinch of salt
- 1 1/2 cups of uncooked quinoa (well-rinsed)
- 1/2 teaspoon (or 1 scoop) of stevia extract
- 1/2 teaspoon of vanilla
- 2 1/4 cups of water

Directions

1. Press the **FISH/VEGETABLES STEAM** button of the pressure cooker. Set the timer to 2 minutes. Put the quinoa, water, salt, vanilla, stevia, salt, and cinnamon in the cooking pot. Lock the lid in place and set the valve to pressure position.
2. Once it is done, the cooker will automatically go to keep warm mode. Turn the valve to the steam position to release pressure.
3. Fluff the quinoa. Top with your preferred toppings before serving.

Crustless Meaty Quiche

Prep time: 30 min
Cook time: 40 min
Servings: 4

Ingredients

- 1 cup of ground sausage (cooked)
- 6 large eggs (beaten)
- 1/2 cup of milk
- 4 slices of bacon (cooked and crumbled)
- 1/8 teaspoon of ground black pepper
- 1/4 teaspoon of salt
- 1/2 cup of diced ham
- 1 cup of shredded cheese
- 2 large green onions (chopped)

Directions

1. Place the trivet at the bottom of the cooker before pouring in 1 1/2 cups of water. Press the **BEANS/LENTILS** button and set the timer to 30 minutes.
2. In a bowl, mix the eggs, milk, pepper, and salt. In a soufflé dish, mix the sausage, ham, bacon, green onions, and cheese. Stir in the egg mixture. Cover it with a loose foil and place it on top of the trivet. Lock the lid in place and set the valve to pressure position.
3. Once it is done, the cooker will automatically go to keep warm mode. Turn the valve to the steam position to release pressure.

Egg Muffins

Prep time: 5 min
Cook time: 8 min
Servings: 4

Ingredients

- 4 slices of bacon (cooked and crumbled)
- 4 eggs, 1 green onion (diced)
- 4 tablespoons of shredded cheddar cheese
- 1/4 teaspoon of lemon pepper seasoning

Directions

1. Put the eggs in a bowl. Add the lemon pepper seasoning and beat until fluffy.
2. Prepare 4 muffin cups. Spoon an equal amount of bacon, cheese, and onion into each cup. Pour the beaten eggs on top of each cup. Use a fork to gently stir.
3. Put the steamer basket inside the pressure cooker. Add 1 1/2 cups of water. Press the **RICE/RISOTTO** button and set the timer to 8 minutes. Place the muffin cups inside the basket. Lock the lid in place and set the valve to pressure position.
4. Once it is done, turn the valve to the steam position to release pressure.

Risotto

Prep time: 3 min
Cook time: 15 min
Servings: 4

Ingredients

- 1 cup of grated Parmesan cheese (divided)
- 1/4 cup olive oil
- 2 cups of Arborio rice
- 1 teaspoon of saffron
- 1/2 cup of wine
- 4 cups of chicken stock
- 1 medium yellow onion (diced)
- 2 tablespoons of butter
- Parsley or thyme as garnishing
- Salt to taste

Directions

1. Heat the stock in a pan over low flame. Simmer while you work with the rest of the ingredients.
2. Press the **CHICKEN/MEAT** button. Wait for the pot to heat up. Add the olive oil. Once the oil is heated, put in the onion and salt. Saute until soft or around 4 minutes. Put in the rice and stir until lightly toasted. Add the saffron and wine. Pour in the heated stock.
3. Press the **RICE/RISOTTO** button. Lock the lid in place and set the valve to pressure position. Once it is done, turn the valve to the steam position to release pressure.
4. Open the lid. Stir in the butter and half of the Parmesan and butter. Season with salt. Garnish with the remaining cheese and herbs before serving.

Nutritious Steel-Cut Oats for Breakfast

Prep time: 20 min
Cook time: 3 min
Servings: 3

Ingredients

- 1/2 tablespoon of raw honey & 1/2 teaspoon of water
- 1/2 tablespoon of butter
- 170 grams of water
- A pinch of salt
- 40 grams of quick-cooking steel-cut oats

Directions

1. Mix the oats, water, salt, and butter in a bowl. Pour 2 cups of water in the pressure cooker pot. Place the steamer basket and put the bowl inside. Press the **FISH/VEGETABLES** steam button. Set the timer to 3 minutes. Lock the lid in place and set the valve to pressure position.
2. Once it is done, turn the valve to the steam position to release pressure.
3. Open the lid. Transfer the cooked oats into serving bowls. Pour the honey mixed with 1/2 teaspoon of water on top before serving.

Cinnamon Raisin Bread Pudding

Prep time: 10 min
Cook time: 20 min
Servings: 6

Ingredients

- 3 eggs (beaten)
- 4 tablespoons of melted butter
- 3 cups of whole milk
- 1/4 cup of raw honey, & 1 tablespoon of water
- 1/2 teaspoon of ground cinnamon
- 1 teaspoon of vanilla extract
- 7 thick slices of cinnamon bread (cubed and toasted)
- 1/2 cup of raisins
- 1/4 teaspoon of salt

For the caramel pecan sauce

- 1/2 teaspoon of salt
- 1/2 cup of toasted and chopped pecans
- 1 teaspoon of vanilla extract
- 2 tablespoons of heavy cream
- 1/32 teaspoon (or 1 scoop) of stevia extract
- 2 tablespoons of butter

Directions

1. Put the beaten eggs in a bowl. Add vanilla, milk, cinnamon, raw honey mixed with water, melted butter, and salt. Mix well. Put in the raisins and bread. Soak for 20 minutes.
2. Pour the bread pudding mixture to a greased baking dish. Cover with foil and put it inside the pressure cooker. Press the **CHICKEN/MEAT** button and set the timer to 20 minutes. Lock the lid in place and set the valve to pressure position.
3. Once it is done, turn the valve to the steam position to release pressure. Open the lid.

4. Prepare the sauce. Heat a saucepan over medium flame. Put in the butter, heavy cream, stevia extract, and salt. Bring to a boil while stirring often. Turn the heat to low. Stir in the vanilla and chopped pecans.
5. Transfer the pudding to a platter. Drizzle the sauce on top before serving.

Scotch Eggs

Prep time: 10 min
Cook time: 15 min
Servings: 4

Ingredients

- 1 pound of ground sausage
- 1 tablespoon of vegetable oil
- 4 large eggs

Directions

1. Press the **RICE/RISOTTO** button of the pressure cooker. Add a cup of water to the pot before placing the steamer basket. Put the eggs inside the basket. Lock the lid in place and set the valve to pressure position. Once it is done, turn the valve to the steam position to release pressure.
2. Open the lid. Put the eggs into a bowl with cold water.
3. Cut the sausage into 4 and flatten each piece. Peel the eggs. Wrap each with the flattened sausage.
4. Press the **SOUP/STEW** button to reset the timer of the pressure cooker to 10 minutes. Heat oil. Put the Scotch eggs and cook until all sides are browned. Transfer them to a platter.
5. Pour a cup of water into the pot. Put the rack inside and arrange the Scotch eggs on top. Press the **RICE/RISOTTO** button. Lock the lid in place and set the valve to pressure position. When the timer is done, turn the valve to the steam position to release pressure.

Carrot Cake Oatmeal

Prep time: 5 min
Cook time: 15 min
Servings: 6

Ingredients

- 1/4 teaspoon each of chia seeds and salt
- 1 cup of steel cut oats
- 2 teaspoons of cinnamon
- 1 cup of grated carrots
- 1 tablespoon of butter
- 1 teaspoon of pumpkin pie spice
- 1/32 teaspoon (or 1 scoop) of stevia extract
- 4 cups of water

Directions

1. Press the **CHICKEN/MEAT** button. Wait for the pot to heat up. Melt butter. Add the oats and toast for 3 minutes. Add water, pumpkin pie spice, carrots, salt, cinnamon, and maple syrup. Lock the lid in place and set the valve to pressure position.
2. Once it is done, the cooker will automatically go to keep warm mode. Turn the valve to the steam position to release pressure. Open the lid. Stir the cooked oats, and then add the raisins and chia seeds. Cover the pot and let it stand for 10 minutes.
3. Transfer into serving bowls. Add the stevia extract and milk. Top with chopped nuts before serving.

Cranberry Orange French Toast

Prep time: 3 min
Cook time: 6 min
Servings: 8

Ingredients

- Grated zest from 1 orange
- 1 teaspoon of vanilla extract
- A loaf of Challah bread (cubed)
- 1/4 teaspoon of salt
- 4 tablespoons of melted butter
- 3 eggs (beaten)
- 1/8 cup of raw honey, & 1 teaspoon of water
- 2 cups whole milk

For the cranberry orange sauce

- 1/8 cup of raw honey, & 1 teaspoon of water
- 2 cups of cranberries (washed)
- 1/4 cup of fresh orange juice
- 1/4 teaspoon each of ground cinnamon and salt

Directions

1. Put the orange juice in a saucepan over medium-high heat. Stir in the cinnamon, salt, honey with water, and cranberries. Cook 5 minutes. Remove from the stove. Transfer the mixture to a baking pan.
2. Combine the melted butter, honey, and a teaspoon of water in a bowl. Whisk in the eggs, salt, milk, orange zest, and vanilla. Soak the cubed bread into the mixture. Pour on top of the cranberry juice in the baking pan.
3. Pour a cup of water in the pot of the pressure cooker. Place the trivet inside and put the baking pan on top. Press the **CHICKEN/MEAT** button and set the timer to 25 minutes. Lock the lid in place and set the valve to pressure position.

4. Once it is done, the cooker will automatically go to keep warm mode. Turn the valve to the steam position to release pressure.

Healthy Chicken Stew

Prep time: 5 min
Cook time: 70 min
Servings: 4

Ingredients

- 2 tomatoes (diced)
- 1/2 cup of parsley (chopped)
- Salt and pepper to taste
- 1 potato (peeled and cubed)
- 5 chicken thighs (skinless)
- 2 carrots (chopped)
- 2 garlic cloves (minced)
- 1 onion (diced)
- 9 cups of chicken stock

Directions

1. Put all the ingredients in the pressure cooker pot. Press the **SOUP/STEW** button and the **COOK TIME SELECTOR** button once to set the timer to 30 minutes. Lock the lid in place and set the valve to pressure position. Once it is done, the cooker will automatically go to keep warm mode. Turn the valve to the steam position to release pressure.

CHAPTER 3

POWER PRESSURE COOKER XL CHICKEN RECIPES

Roasted Chicken

Prep time: 5 min
Cook time: 70 min
Servings: 4

Ingredients

- 6 pounds of whole chicken
- Salt and pepper to taste
- 2 cups of baby carrots
- 3 cups of baby potatoes

Directions

1. Press the **CHICKEN/MEAT** button. Wait for the pot to heat up. Put in the chicken and cook until seared. Add the remaining ingredients.
2. Press the **KEEP WARM/CANCEL** button to reset the timer. Press the **CHICKEN/MEAT** button. Press the **COOK TIME SELECTOR** button twice and adjust the time to 70 minutes by pressing the **TIME ADJUSTMENT** button. Lock the lid in place and set the valve to pressure position. Once it is done, the cooker will automatically go to keep warm mode. Turn the valve to the steam position to release pressure.

Chicken Parmesan Meatballs

Prep time: 10 min
Cook time: 20 min
Servings: 4

Ingredients

- 1 14-ounce can of chicken broth
- 1 pound of ground chicken
- 2 tablespoons each of cornstarch and onion (finely chopped)
- 1/2 cup of grated Parmesan cheese
- 2 ounces of cream cheese
- 1/3 cup of sour cream
- 1/4 teaspoon each of salt and pepper
- 1 garlic clove (minced)
- 1/3 cup of seasoned breadcrumbs
- 3 tablespoons of water
- 1 egg (beaten)
- 1 tablespoon each of vegetable oil and chopped parsley
- 1 teaspoon of lemon juice
- 2 teaspoons of ranch dressing seasoning mix

Directions

1. Put the meat in a bowl. Add the breadcrumbs, egg, parsley, cheese, salt, pepper, onion, and garlic. Use your hands to turn them into small meatballs. Put them in a tray, cover with plastic and refrigerate for half an hour.
2. Pour the chicken broth into the pressure cooker pot. Add the ranch dressing seasoning mix and stir. Place the greased trivet inside the pot. Put the meatballs on top. Press the **SOUP/STEW** button to set the timer to 10 minutes. Lock the lid in place and set the valve to pressure position. Once it is done, turn the valve to the steam position to release pressure. Open the lid. Transfer the meatballs to a plate. Remove the trivet and keep the cooking liquid.
3. Put vegetable oil in a heated skillet over high flame. Put in the pressure cooked meatballs and brown all sides.

4. Press the **KEEP WARM/CANCEL** button to reset the timer of the pressure cooker. Choose the **SOUP/STEW** button. Bring the broth to a boil. Add the cream cheese and the mixture of cornstarch and water. Simmer while stirring often. Stir in the lemon juice and sour cream.
5. Place the meatballs on a platter and drizzle with the sauce. Let it stand for 5 minutes. Top with parsley before serving.

Korean Chicken Thighs

Prep time: 15 min
Cook time: 30 min
Servings: 6

Ingredients

- 1 cup of chicken broth
- 2 pounds of chicken thighs (bone-in and with the skin removed)
- 2 teaspoons of cornstarch
- 2 tablespoons of vegetable oil
- 1 onion (chopped)
- 1 teaspoon of garlic (minced)
- 1 tablespoon of ginger (minced)
- 1/4 cup of broth or water

For the Korean barbecue sauce

- 1/2 cup of gochujang
- 1/4 cup each of ketchup, soy sauce, hoisin sauce, sake rice wine and mirin
- 1/2 tablespoon of garlic (minced)
- 1 tablespoon each of unseasoned rice vinegar and fresh ginger (minced)

Directions

1. Whisk all the ingredients for the sauce in a bowl. Set aside 1 cup.
2. Press the **CHICKEN/MEAT** button of your Power Pressure Cooker. Wait for the pot to heat up. Put the vegetable oil, add the meat and cook until browned. Transfer the chicken to a platter. Add the onion, ginger, and garlic to the pot. Saute for 3 minutes. Put back the browned chicken pieces. Add the chicken broth and the remaining sauce in the bowl.
3. Press the **KEEP WARM/CANCEL** button of the pressure cooker to reset the timer. Press the **Chicken/Meat** button. Lock the lid in place and set the valve to pressure position. Once it is done, turn the valve to the steam position to release pressure. Open the lid.

Add the mixture of cornstarch and water. Stir until the sauce thickens. Stir in the reserved sauce.

Orange Chicken

Prep time: 3 min
Cook time: 6 min
Servings: 6

Ingredients

- 3 tablespoons of cornstarch (dissolved in 3 tablespoons of water)
- 4 large chicken breasts (boneless, skinless, and diced)
- 1 teaspoon of sesame oil
- 1/4 teaspoon chili garlic sauce
- 1/32 teaspoon (or 1 scoop) of stevia extract
- 1/4 cup each of water and soy sauce
- 1 tablespoon of rice wine vinegar
- 1/2 cup of orange marmalade

Directions

1. Press the **FISH/VEGETABLES STEAM** button of the pressure cooker. Set the timer to 3 minutes. Put the meat into the pot. Add water, stevia extract, rice wine vinegar, chili garlic sauce, and sesame oil. Lock the lid in place and set the valve to pressure position.
2. Once it is done, the cooker will automatically go to keep warm mode. Turn the valve to the steam position to release pressure. Open the lid. Stir in the dissolved cornstarch in water and marmalade. Press any preset button. Simmer the sauce until it thickens.

Savory Chicken with Honey and Nuts

Prep time: 5 min
Cook time: 10 min
Servings: 6

Ingredients

- 4 large chicken breasts (skinless, boneless, and diced)
- 2 green onions (chopped)
- 1 tablespoon of vegetable oil
- 1/2 cup each of soy sauce and onion (diced)
- 2 cloves of garlic (minced)
- 2 tablespoons of cornstarch
- 3 tablespoons of water
- Salt and pepper to taste
- 1/4 teaspoon of red pepper flakes
- 1 cup of raw honey, & 4 tablespoons of water
- 2 teaspoons of sesame oil
- 1/4 cup of ketchup
- Chopped nuts of your choice

Directions

1. Season the meat with salt and pepper. Press the **CHICKEN/MEAT** button of your pressure cooker. Wait for the pot to heat up. Add oil. Saute the onion, garlic and seasoned chicken for 3 minutes. Add the ketchup, red pepper flakes, and soy sauce.
2. Press the **KEEP WARM/CANCEL** button to reset the timer. Press the **FISH/VEGETABLES STEAM** button and set the timer to 3 minutes. Lock the lid in place and set the valve to pressure position. Once it is done, turn the valve to the steam position to release pressure.
3. Open the lid. Add sesame oil and the honey mixed with water. Give it a quick stir. Dissolve cornstarch in water and add this to the mixture. Press any preset button of the pressure cooker. Stir the sauce until thick and add the green onions.
4. Transfer to a bowl. Top with chopped nuts before serving.

Chicken Wings in Teriyaki Sauce

Prep time: 10 min
Cook time: 20 min
Servings: 3

Ingredients

- 1/2 cup of teriyaki sauce
- 2 pounds of chicken drumettes and wings

Directions

1. Press the **BEANS/LENTILS** button of the pressure cooker. Set the timer to 5 minutes. Add a cup of water to the cooker. Put the trivet inside. Arrange the meat on top of the trivet. Lock the lid in place and set the valve to pressure position. Once it is done, turn the valve to the steam position to release pressure.
2. Open the lid. Pat the meat dry using paper towels. Put them in a bowl and season with teriyaki sauce. Mix well. Transfer to a baking tray. Bake for 15 minutes in a preheated oven at 450 degrees.

Chicken Marsala

Prep time: 10 min
Cook time: 20 min
Servings: 4

Ingredients

- 1/2 cup of sweet Marsala wine
- 3 pounds of chicken thighs (skinless, boneless, and trimmed)
- 1 tablespoon of vegetable oil
- 1 cup of chicken broth
- Salt and pepper to taste
- 2 tablespoons of cornstarch (dissolved in 3 tablespoons of cold water)
- 8 ounces of mushrooms (sliced)
- 3 tablespoons of butter (divided)
- 2 tablespoons of chopped parsley
- 4 slices of peppered bacon (diced)
- Chopped parsley or chives for garnish

Directions

1. Press the **CHICKEN/MEAT** button of your pressure cooker. Wait for the pot to heat up. Put in the bacon and cook until brown and crisp. Transfer them to a plate and leave the drippings on the pot.
2. Season the meat with salt and pepper before putting them inside the pot. Cook until all sides are browned. Transfer to a platter.
3. Add the marsala to the pot. Once heated, pour the chicken broth and stir. Put the browned meat back into the pot. Press the **SOUP/STEW** button to set the timer to 10 minutes. Lock the lid in place and set the valve to pressure position. Once it is done, turn the valve to the steam position to release pressure. Transfer the meat to a plate.
4. Heat oil and 1 tablespoon of butter in a saucepan over medium-high flame. Add the mushrooms and cook until golden. Season with salt and pepper.

5. Add the dissolved cornstarch mixture to the pot. Simmer while stirring frequently. Add the cooked mushrooms and the remaining butter.
6. Pour the sauce on top of the chicken with sauce before serving. Sprinkle with crumbled bacon to garnish.

Indian Butter Chicken

Prep time: 15 min
Cook time: 30 min
Servings: 8

Ingredients

- 10 pieces of chicken thighs (skinless, boneless, and quartered)
- 2 jalapeno peppers (seeded and chopped)
- 1/4 cup of firmly packed cilantro (minced)
- 2 teaspoons of each ground cumin seeds (toasted), kosher salt, and garam masala
- A stick of unsalted butter
- 2 14-ounce cans of diced tomatoes and juice
- 1 tablespoon of paprika
- 2 tablespoons of fresh ginger root (peeled and chopped)
- 2 tablespoons of cornstarch (dissolved in 2 tablespoons of water)
- 3/4 cup each of heavy cream and Greek yogurt

Directions

1. Put jalapeno, tomatoes, and ginger in a food processor. Process until pureed.
2. Press the **CHICKEN/MEAT** button of your pressure cooker. Wait for the pot to heat up. Melt the butter. Put in the meat and sear until all sides are browned. Transfer to a platter and set aside.
3. Add the ground cumin and paprika to the pot. Stir for 15 seconds. Put back the chicken. Stir in the yogurt, cream, salt, and tomato mixture. Press the **BEANS/LENTILS** button to set the timer to 5 minutes. Lock the lid in place and set the valve to pressure position. Once it is done, turn the valve to the steam position to release pressure.
4. Add the dissolved cornstarch, garam masala, and roasted cumin. Press the **CHICKEN/MEAT** button. Bring the mixture to a boil. Add the minced cilantro and serve.

Braised Chicken

Prep time: 15 min
Cook time: 30 min
Servings: 4

Ingredients

- 4 chicken breasts (skinless and bone-in)
- Salt to taste
- 1 can of chicken broth
- 1/2 cup of minced flat-leaf parsley
- 2 tablespoons of olive oil (divided)
- 1/3 cup each of salted capers (soaked well) and white wine vinegar
- 1 large onion (minced)
- 1 tablespoon of cornstarch (dissolved in a tablespoon of water)
- Freshly ground black pepper

Directions

1. Press the **CHICKEN/MEAT** button of your pressure cooker. Wait for the pot to heat up. Put 1 tablespoon of oil into the pot. Season the chicken breasts with salt and pepper before adding them to the pot. Cook until all sides of the meat are browned. Transfer them to a plate. Add the remaining oil to the pot. Cook the onion for 5 minutes. Add the parsley and capers. Cook for a minute. Add the broth and put the browned meat back to the pot.
2. Press the **KEEP WARM/CANCEL** button to reset the timer. Press the **SOUP/STEW** button. Lock the lid in place and set the valve to pressure position. Once it is done, turn the valve to the steam position to release pressure.
3. Open the lid. Put chicken into a plate and cover it with loose foil. Put the dissolved cornstarch into the pot. Reset the timer to 10 minutes. Bring to a boil while stirring often. Season with salt and pepper.
4. Pour the sauce on top of the chicken before serving.

Creamy Chicken with Broccoli

Prep time: 10 min
Cook time: 20 min
Servings: 3-6

Ingredients

- 2 large chicken breasts (boneless and skinless)
- 1 cup of cheddar cheese
- 4 ounces of light cream cheese (cubed)
- 1 tablespoon each of butter, dried parsley, and olive oil
- 3 cups of broccoli (chopped and lightly steamed)
- 1/2 cup of chopped onion
- 1 can of chicken broth
- 2 tablespoons of cornstarch (dissolved in 2 tablespoons of water)
- 1/8 teaspoon of red pepper flakes
- 1/2 teaspoon each of black pepper and salt

Directions

1. Press the **CHICKEN/MEAT** button of your pressure cooker. Wait for the pot to heat up. Melt the butter and add oil to the pot. Season the chicken breasts with salt and pepper before adding them to the pot. Cook the meat until all sides are browned. Transfer them to a plate. Add the onion to the pot. Saute for 5 minutes. Add the chicken broth, parsley, and red pepper flakes. Put back the browned chicken to the pot. Give it a quick stir.
2. Press the **BEANS/LENTILS** button of the pressure cooker. Lock the lid in place and set the valve to pressure position. Open the lid. Put the chicken onto a cutting board and chop into smaller pieces.
3. Press the **KEEP WARM/CANCEL** button to reset the timer. Choose the **SOUP/STEW** button to set the time to 10 minutes. Simmer the sauce. Add the cream cheese, shredded cheese, and dissolved cornstarch. Once the cheese melts, put back the meat into the pot. Add the broccoli and simmer for 5 more minutes.

CHAPTER 4

POWER PRESSURE COOKER XL BEEF RECIPES

Pot Roast

Prep time: 30 min
Cook time: 1 hour and 30 mins
Servings: 6

Ingredients

- 1 1/2 cup of beef broth
- 3 1/2 pounds of rump roast
- 1 large onion (chopped)
- 1 tablespoon of vegetable oil
- 2 bay leaves

Directions

1. Pat the roast with paper towels to dry. Season it with lemon pepper.
2. Press the **CHICKEN/MEAT** button of your pressure cooker. Wait for the pot to heat up. Add the oil. Put in the meat and brown all sides. Transfer the browned meat to a plate. Put the onions into the pot. Saute for 5 minutes. Add the broth and bay leaves. Put the meat back into the pot.
3. Press the **KEEP WARM/CANCEL** button to reset the timer. Press the **CHICKEN/MEAT** button once and the **COOK TIME SELECTOR** button twice. Add 10 more minutes to the time by pressing the **TIME ADJUSTMENT** button. This will set the cook time to 70 minutes. Lock the lid in place and set the valve to pressure position. Once it is done, turn the valve to the steam position to release pressure.

4. Open the lid. Transfer the roast to a platter. Strain the cooking liquid and put it back into the pot. Simmer the liquid until thick.
5. Serve the meat along with the sauce.

Spicy Orange Beef

Prep time: 10 min
Cook time: 20 min
Servings: 8

Ingredients

- 2 pounds of flank steak (cut into strips)
- 2 tablespoons of cornstarch dissolved in 3 tablespoons of cold water
- 6 cloves of garlic (minced)
- 1 bunch of green onions (sliced)
- 1 teaspoon of orange zest
- 1 tablespoon of vegetable oil
- 2 teaspoons of sesame oil
- 1/4 cup of soy sauce
- 3/4 cup of fresh orange juice
- 1/2 teaspoon of red pepper flakes

Directions

1. Press the **CHICKEN/MEAT** button of your pressure cooker. Put the oil into the pot once it heats up. Season the meat with salt and pepper. Brown them in batches. Transfer the browned meat to a plate. Put garlic in the pot. Saute for 1 minute. Add the red pepper flakes, sesame oil, orange zest, orange juice, and soy sauce. Put the meat back into the pot.
2. Press the **KEEP WARM/CANCEL** button to reset the timer. Choose the **SOUP/STEW** button to set the time to 10 minutes. Lock the lid in place and set the valve to pressure position. Once it is done, turn the valve to the steam position to release pressure.
3. Simmer the dish. Add the dissolved cornstarch. Stir until thick. Turn off the cooker and add the green onions.

Sloppy Lasagna

Prep time: 15 min
Cook time: 35 min
Servings: 6

Ingredients

- 8 ounces of mozzarella cheese (diced)
- 8 ounces of wavy lasagna noodles (broken into small pieces)
- Water (as needed)
- 1 teaspoon of salt

For the meat ragu sauce
- 1 pound of ground beef chuck
- 1 sprig each of fresh thyme and fresh oregano
- 2 garlic cloves (crushed)
- 1 tablespoon of olive oil
- 1/4 teaspoon of freshly ground black pepper
- 1/2 teaspoon of salt
- 1/2 cup of tomato puree
- 1 cup of chopped tomatoes
- 1 carrot (chopped)
- 2 tablespoons of unsalted butter
- 1 yellow onion (chopped)
- 1 celery stick (chopped)

Directions

1. Prepare the sauce. Press the **CHICKEN/MEAT** button of your pressure cooker. Wait for the pot to heat up. Put in 1 tablespoon of butter and olive oil. Add the onion, salt, pepper, thyme, and oregano. Stir for 5 minutes. Add the carrots and celery. Push them to one side of the cooking pot. Put in the meat and add the garlic. Cook for 5 minutes. Put in the tomatoes.
2. Press the **KEEP WARM/CANCEL** button to reset the timer. Press the **BEANS/LENTILS** button. Lock the lid in place and set the

valve to pressure position. Once it is done, turn the valve to the steam position to release pressure.

3. Open the lid. Remove the stems of the herbs. Stir in the remaining butter. Put in the lasagna strips. Season with salt. Add 1 cup of water. Reset the timer to 5 minutes. Lock the lid in place and set the valve to pressure position. Turn the valve to the steam position to release pressure once the timer is done.

4. Top the dish with mozzarella cheese before serving.

Smokey Beef Brisket

Prep time: 30 min
Cook time: 1 hour and 15 min
Servings: 6

Ingredients

- 3 pounds of flat-cut beef brisket (trim excess fat)
- 1/4 teaspoon each of garlic salt, seasoned salt, and celery salt
- 2 tablespoons of liquid smoke
- 1/2 cup of water
- 1 tablespoon of Worcestershire sauce
- 1 teaspoon of seasoned meat tenderizer
- 1 cup of barbecue sauce (add more for serving)

Directions

1. In a bowl, combine the meat tenderizer and the three kinds of salt. Season the brisket with the mixture. Put the seasoned meat in a Ziploc bag. Add the liquid smoke and Worcestershire sauce. Seal the bag and leave in the fridge to marinate overnight.
2. Put the brisket and the juices into the pot of the pressure cooker. Add water and the barbecue sauce. Press the **CHICKEN/MEAT** button of the pressure cooker once and the **COOK TIME SELECTOR** button twice to set timer to 60 minutes. Lock the lid in place and set the valve to pressure position. Once it is done, turn the valve to the steam position to release pressure.
3. Open the lid. Put the meat on a platter and slice before serving.

Beef Stroganoff

Prep time: 15 min
Cook time: 45 min
Servings: 8

Ingredients

- 2 pounds of beef round steak (cut into bite-size pieces)
- 2 garlic cloves (minced)
- 1 onion (chopped)
- 2 tablespoons of cornstarch dissolved in 3 tablespoons of cold water
- 1 pack of white mushrooms (sliced)
- 2 tablespoons of tomato paste
- Salt and pepper to taste
- 1 1/2 cups of beef broth
- 1 tablespoon each of butter and vegetable oil
- 1/3 cup of sour cream
- Egg noodles (cooked)

Directions

1. Press the **CHICKEN/MEAT** button of your pressure cooker. Wait for the pot to heat up. Add oil. Season the meat with salt and pepper. Brown it in batches. Transfer the browned meat onto a plate. Put the onion into the pot and saute for 5 minutes. Add the garlic and tomato paste. Cook for 1 minute. Add the beef broth and put the browned meat back into the pot.
2. Press the **KEEP WARM/CANCEL** button to reset the timer. Press the **CHICKEN/MEAT** button and set the timer to 18 minutes. Lock the lid in place and set the valve to pressure position. Once it is done, turn the valve to the steam position to release pressure.
3. Heat butter and oil in a saucepan over medium-high flame. Add the mushrooms and cook until golden. Season with salt and pepper.
4. Open the lid of the pressure cooker. Add the dissolved cornstarch to the pot. Simmer the sauce and bring to a boil. Add the mushrooms and sour cream. Mix until blended.
5. Put the cooked noodles in a bowl. Pour the beef stroganoff on top.

Barbecue Bacon Meatloaf

Prep time: 10 min
Cook time: 25 min
Servings: 8

Ingredients

- 3 eggs (beaten)
- 2 pounds of ground beef
- 3 slices of bread
- 8 bacon slices
- Freshly ground black pepper
- 3/4 cup of grated Parmesan cheese
- 2 tablespoons of dried parsley
- 1/2 cup each of milk and barbecue sauce (divided)
- 1 teaspoon of salt
- 1/4 teaspoon of seasoned salt

Directions

1. Put the milk in a bowl. Add the bread and leave it there until soaked. Add the ground beef, eggs, seasoned salt, salt, cheese, black pepper, and parsley. Mix all the ingredients using your hands. Turn it into the shape of a loaf. Place it at the center of a foil sling. Put the bacon slices on top. Drizzle 1/4 cup of the barbecue sauce on top.
2. Pour 2 cups of water in the pressure cooker pot. Place the trivet inside and put the meatloaf on top. Press the **CHICKEN/MEAT** button of the pressure cooker. Set the timer to 20 minutes. Lock the lid in place and set the valve to pressure position. Once it is done, turn the valve to the steam position to release pressure.
3. Open the lid. Put the meatloaf in a broiler pan. Add the rest of the barbecue sauce. Broil for 5 minutes.

Bone-In Beef Short Ribs

Prep time: 20 min
Cook time: 1 hour and 10 min
Servings: 4

Ingredients

- 2 bacon slices (chopped)
- 4 large beef short ribs
- 3 cloves of garlic (minced)
- 1 onion (finely chopped)
- 1 cup of beef both
- 1/2 cup of apple juice
- 1 tablespoon of cornstarch dissolved in a tablespoon of water
- 2 tablespoons each of tomato paste and vegetable oil

Directions

1. Press the **CHICKEN/MEAT** button of your pressure cooker. Wait for the pot to heat up. Add oil. Season the meat with salt and pepper, and cook it in batches until browned. Transfer the browned meat to a plate. Put the bacon into the pot and cook until crisp. Put in the onion and saute for 3 minutes. Add the garlic and cook for 1 minute. Add the broth, tomato paste, and apple juice.
2. Press the **KEEP WARM/CANCEL** button to reset the timer. Press the **CHICKEN/MEAT** button and the **COOK TIME SELECTOR** button once to set the timer to 40 minutes. Lock the lid in place and set the valve to pressure position. Once it is done, turn the valve to the steam position to release pressure.
3. Open the lid. Put the ribs on a platter. Separate juices from the fat. Put back the juices into the pot. Add the dissolved cornstarch and simmer the sauce until thick. Put back the meat into the pot. Close the lid and leave it for 10 minutes, after which, you can open the lid and stir the sauce.

Corned Beef with Cabbage

Prep time: 30 min
Cook time: 1 hour and 40 min
Servings: 6

Ingredients

- 4 cups of beef broth
- 3 pounds of flat-cut corned beef brisket (with seasoning packet, rinsed with cold water)
- 1 cabbage (cut into 6 wedges)
- 8 cloves of garlic
- 6 red potatoes (quartered)
- 1 onion (quartered)
- 3 carrots (sliced)

Directions

1. Pour the beef broth into the pot of the pressure cooker. Add the garlic, onion, and the seasoning packet. Put in the rack and place the corned beef on top. Press the **CHICKEN/MEAT** button and the **COOK TIME SELECTOR** button twice. Add more 30 minutes to the time by pressing the **TIME ADJUSTMENT** button. Lock the lid in place and set the valve to pressure position.
2. Once it is done, the cooker will automatically go to keep warm mode. Turn the valve to the steam position to release pressure. Open the lid. Remove the rack and transfer the meat onto a plate. Cover it with a loose foil to retain the heat.
3. Add the potatoes and cabbage to the broth. Press the **FISH/VEGETABLES STEAM** button and set the timer to 3 minutes. Lock the lid in place and set the valve to pressure position. Turn the valve to the steam position to release pressure once the timer is done.
4. Serve the meat along with hot soup.

Shredded Beef Enchiladas

Prep time: 30 min
Cook time: 2 hours
Servings: 10

Ingredients

- 10 6-inch corn or flour tortillas
- 1 3-pound chuck beef roast
- 1 cup of salsa
- 1/2 teaspoon of pepper
- 1 teaspoon each of chili powder, garlic powder, salt, ground cumin, and onion powder
- 1 1/2 cups each of shredded Mexican cheese blend and beef broth
- 2 tablespoons of apple cider vinegar
- 2 tablespoons of cornstarch dissolved in 3 tablespoons of water

Directions

1. Combine the broth, vinegar, onion powder, cumin, garlic powder, salsa, chili powder, salt, and pepper in the pot of the pressure cooker. Add the meat. Press the **CHICKEN/MEAT** button. Press the **COOK TIME SELECTOR** button twice and adjust the time to 75 minutes by pressing the **TIME ADJUSTMENT** button. Lock the lid in place and set the valve to pressure position. Once it is done, turn the valve to the steam position to release pressure.
2. Open the lid. Transfer the meat to a plate. Shred it using two forks. Remove the fat as you work on the meat.
3. Put the dissolved cornstarch into the pot. Stir the sauce until thick. Add 1/2 cup of the sauce to the shredded meat.
4. Spread 1/2 cup of the sauce in the greased baking pan.
5. Lay a tortilla on a flat surface. Fill the tortilla with 1/3 cup of the beef mixture and a tablespoon of cheese. Roll and put it in the pan. Follow the same steps until you are done with all the tortillas. Pour the rest of the sauce and add the remaining cheese on top. Bake for 30 minutes in a preheated oven at 350 degrees.

Stuffed Green Pepper Casserole

Prep time: 5 min
Cook time: 15 min
Servings: 6

Ingredients

- 1 8-ounce can of tomato sauce
- 1 pound of lean ground beef
- 1/2 cup each of long grain rice (uncooked), chopped onion, and beef broth
- 1 14.5-ounce can of diced tomatoes with juices
- 1 cup of shredded mozzarella cheese
- 2 cloves of garlic (minced)
- 1 tablespoon of Worcestershire sauce
- A handful of spinach leaves (chopped)
- 2 green peppers (chopped)
- 1/2 teaspoon of salt
- 1/4 teaspoon of pepper

Directions

1. Press the **CHICKEN/MEAT** button of your pressure cooker. Wait for the pot to heat up. Add the meat and onion. Cook until browned. Add the garlic and cook for a minute. Put in the broth. Add the green peppers, tomato sauce, tomatoes, spinach, rice, and Worcestershire sauce. Season with salt and pepper.
2. Press the **KEEP WARM/CANCEL** button to reset the timer. Press the **FISH/VEGETABLES STEAM** button and set the timer to 4 minutes. Lock the lid in place and set the valve to pressure position. Once it is done, turn the valve to the steam position to release pressure.
3. Transfer the dish onto a baking pan. Add cheese on top. Broil for a couple of minutes or until the cheese melts.

CHAPTER 5

POWER PRESSURE COOKER XL PORK RECIPES

Bone-In Pork Chops with Carrots and Cauliflower

Prep time: 5 min
Cook time: 10 min
Servings: 4

Ingredients

- 1/4 cup grass-fed butter (divided)
- Salt and pepper to taste
- 1 cup of baby carrots
- 4 3/4-inch thick bone in pork chops
- 2 cups of cauliflower florets
- 1 cup of vegetable broth
- 3 tablespoons Worcestershire sauce
- 1 onion (chopped)

Directions

1. Press the **CHICKEN/MEAT** button of your pressure cooker. Melt 2 tablespoons of butter in the pot. Season the pork chops with salt and pepper, and cook them in batches until browned. Transfer them to a plate.
2. Add the remaining butter to the pot. Put in the carrots and onion. Saute for 2 minutes. Put in the broth and Worcestershire sauce. Put the browned pork chops back into the pot. Put the steamer basket inside the pot. Place the cauliflower florets in the basket. Press the

SOUP/STEW button. Lock the lid in place and set the valve to pressure position.

3. Once it is done, the cooker will automatically go to keep warm mode. Turn the valve to the steam position to release pressure. Open the lid. Put the cooked veggies and meat on a platter, and serve along with the sauce.

Pork Sirloin Tip Roast

Prep time: 5 min
Cook time: 25 min
Servings: 6-8

Ingredients

- 1/2 cup of apple juice
- 3 pounds of pork sirloin tip roast
- 1 tablespoon of vegetable oil
- 1/2 teaspoon each of onion powder, salt, garlic powder, and coarse black pepper
- 1/4 teaspoon of chili powder
- 1 cup of water

Directions

1. Combine the spices in a bowl. Season the meat with the spice blend. Press the **CHICKEN/MEAT** button of your pressure cooker. Heat oil and cook the meat until browned. Add the apple juice and water.
2. Press the **KEEP WARM/CANCEL** button to reset the timer. Press the **RICE/RISOTTO** button of the pressure cooker. Press the **COOK TIME SELECTOR** button twice to set the timer to 25 minutes. Lock the lid in place and set the valve to pressure position. Turn the valve to the steam position to release pressure once it is done cooking.

Pork and Hominy Stew

Prep time: 3 min
Cook time: 30 min
Servings: 8

Ingredients

- 1 1/4 pounds of boneless pork shoulder (trimmed and chopped)
- 4 cups of chicken broth (divided)
- 2 tablespoons each of vegetable oil (divided) and chili powder
- 4 garlic cloves (minced)
- Coarse salt
- 1 white onion (chopped)
- 2 29-ounce cans of hominy (rinsed and drained)
- 2 tablespoons of arrowroot starch (dissolved in 1/4 cup of cold water)

Directions

1. Press the **CHICKEN/MEAT** button of your pressure cooker. Cook the meat until browned. Transfer the browned meat to a plate. Saute the garlic, chili powder, and chopped onion for 4 minutes. Put the meat back in and add the broth. Press the **SOUP/STEW** button and the **COOK TIME SELECTOR** once to set the timer to 30 minutes. Lock the lid in place and set the valve to pressure position. Turn the valve to the steam position to release pressure once the timer is done.
2. Open the lid. Shred the meat. Add the arrowroot starch mixture and hominy to the pot. Stir to combine. Season with salt and pepper.

Pork Carnitas

Prep time: 5 min
Cook time: 1 hour and 5 min
Servings: 10-12

Ingredients

- 3 pounds of pork shoulder (cut into small cubes)
- Juice from 1 lemon
- 2 teaspoons each of kosher salt, hot chili sauce, and chili powder
- 1 teaspoon each of oregano, cumin, onion powder, and garlic powder
- 1 1/2 cups of water
- 1 bay leaf

Directions

1. Add water to the pressure cooker pot. Put in the meat and bay leaf. Press the **MEAT/CHICKEN** button and the **COOK TIME SELECTOR** button once. Press the **TIME ADJUSTMENT** button to set the timer to 45 minutes. Lock the lid in place and set the valve to pressure position. Turn the valve to the steam position to release pressure once it is done cooking.
2. Open the lid. Discard the bay leaf. Spoon half of the liquid and transfer to a container. Refrigerate and use in another recipe. Stir the sauce and simmer for 20 minutes. Stir in the remaining ingredients.

Pork Chops in Mushroom Gravy

Prep time: 2 min
Cook time: 18 min
Servings: 4

Ingredients

- 2 tablespoons of vegetable oil
- 4 thick bone-in pork chops
- 1 can of condensed cream of mushroom soup
- 1 1/2 cups of water
- Lemon pepper

Directions

1. Season the meat with lemon pepper. Press the **CHICKEN/MEAT** button of your pressure cooker. Brown the pork chops in the pot and transfer them onto a plate. Pour the mushroom soup into the pot and put the meat back in. Press the **KEEP WARM/CANCEL** button to reset the timer. Press the **MEAT/CHICKEN** button and set the timer to 18 minutes. Lock the lid in place and set the valve to pressure position. Turn the valve to the steam position to release pressure once the timer is done.
2. Serve the meat with the gravy on the side.

Pulled Pork

Prep time: 5 min
Cook time: 1 hour 30 min
Servings: 5

Ingredients

- 2 cups of barbecue sauce (divided)
- 1/2 cup of water
- 4 pounds of boneless pork shoulder (cut into two)
- 2 tablespoons of vegetable oil

Directions

1. Press the **CHICKEN/MEAT** button of your pressure cooker. Brown the meat in the pot and transfer to a plate. Add the rest of the ingredients, stir, and put the browned meat back into the pot.
2. Press the **KEEP WARM/CANCEL** button to reset the timer. Press the **CHICKEN/MEAT** button and the **COOK TIME SELECTOR** twice. Press the **TIME ADJUSTMENT** button to adjust cook time to 90 minutes. Lock the lid in place and set the valve to pressure position. Turn the valve to the steam position to release pressure once the timer is done.
3. Open the lid. Shred the meat and reserve half of the cooking liquid. Put in the remaining barbecue sauce and the cooking liquid. Simmer for a couple of minutes.

Egg Roll Soup

Prep time: 2 min
Cook time: 23 min
Servings: 5

Ingredients

- 4 cups of broth (beef or chicken)
- 1 pound of ground pastured pork
- 1 teaspoon each of sea salt, onion powder, ground ginger, and garlic powder
- 2 cups of shredded carrots
- 1/2 head cabbage (chopped)
- 2/3 cup of coconut aminos
- 1 onion (diced)
- 1 tablespoon of olive oil

Directions

1. Press the **CHICKEN/MEAT** button of your pressure cooker. Brown the meat in the pot. Add the onion and saute. Put in the rest of the ingredients. Press the **KEEP WARM/CANCEL** button to reset the timer. Press the **CHICKEN/MEAT** button and set the timer to 23 minutes. Lock the lid in place and set the valve to pressure position. Once it is done, turn the valve to the steam position to release pressure.

Pressure Cooked Kalua Pig

Prep time: 5 min
Cook time: 1 hour and 35 min
Servings: 8

Ingredients

- 5 garlic cloves (peeled)
- 1 cabbage (cored and sliced into 6 wedges)
- 1 1/2 tablespoons of sea salt
- 1 cup of water
- 3 bacon slices
- 5 pounds of bone-in pork shoulder roast

Directions

1. Divide the meat into three. Cut slits and place the garlic cloves inside. Season with salt. Press the **CHICKEN/MEAT** button of your pressure cooker. Saute the bacon in the pot once it heats up. Add the seasoned meat. Add the water to the pot. Press the **KEEP WARM/CANCEL** button to reset the timer. Press the **CHICKEN/MEAT** button and the **COOK TIME SELECTOR** button once. Add 30 more minutes by continuously pressing the **TIME ADJUSTMENT** button until the cook time is set at 90 minutes. Lock the lid in place and set the valve to pressure position. Once it is done, turn the valve to the steam position to release pressure.

2. Open the lid. Transfer the meat to a bowl. Add the cabbage wedges into the pot. Add water as needed. Press the **BEANS/LENTILS** button. Lock the lid in place and set the valve to pressure position. Turn the valve to the steam position to release pressure once the timer is done. Open the lid. Serve the meat with the cabbage on top.

Pork Chops with Onions, Figs, and Balsamic

Prep time: 2 min
Cook time: 7 min
Servings: 4

Ingredients

- 3 tablespoons of aged balsamic vinegar
- 10 ounces of dried figs
- 4 pork bone-in loin chops (well-trimmed)
- 1/2 teaspoon of freshly ground pepper
- 1 teaspoon of kosher salt (divided)
- 1 teaspoon of thyme
- 1/3 cup of chicken stock
- 3 cups of sliced onions
- 2 garlic cloves (chopped)
- 1/2 tablespoon each of unsalted butter and olive oil
- 2 tablespoons of dry white wine

Directions

1. Season the meat. Press the **CHICKEN/MEAT** button of your pressure cooker. Brown the meat in the pot and transfer to a plate. Saute the thyme, onion, and garlic in the pot for 4 minutes. Add the wine and chicken stock. Cook for 1 minute and season with salt and pepper. Put the meat back into the pot. Add the figs.
2. Press the **KEEP WARM/CANCEL** button to reset the timer. Press the beans/lentils button. Set the timer to 7 minutes. Once it is done, turn the valve to the steam position to release pressure.
3. Open the lid. Simmer the sauce. Serve the meat, onions, and figs with the sauce.

Honey Orange Pork

Prep time: 5 min
Cook time: 15 min
Servings: 2-4

Ingredients

- 1 orange
- 2 tablespoons of light soy sauce
- 3 garlic cloves (finely chopped)
- 1 1/2 pounds of pork shoulder meat
- 2 cloves
- A pinch of dried rosemary
- 1 onion (chopped)
- 1 cinnamon stick
- 1 tablespoon each of sliced ginger and grapeseed oil
- 1/2 tablespoon of raw honey (mixed with 2 tablespoons of water)
- 1/2 cup of water
- Salt and pepper to taste
- Dissolved 1 1/2 tablespoons of cornstarch in 1 tablespoon of water

Directions

1. Season the meat. Press the **CHICKEN/MEAT** button of your pressure cooker. Brown the seasoned meat in the pot. Transfer the meat to a plate. Saute the ginger, garlic, and onions. Season with salt and pepper.
    Squeeze half of the orange in the pot. Use a wooden spoon to deglaze the bottom of the pot. Add the light soy sauce, water, cinnamon stick, cloves, dried rosemary, and the honey mixture. Cut the squeezed orange in smaller pieces and put them in the pot.

    Put the meat back into the pot. Press the **KEEP WARM/CANCEL** button to reset the timer. Press the **CHICKEN/MEAT** button and **COOK TIME SELECTOR** once. Add 10 more minutes by pressing the **TIME ADJUSTMENT** button until the cook time is set at 50 minutes. Lock the lid in place and set the valve to pressure position.

Turn the valve to the steam position to release pressure once the timer is done.

2. Open the lid. Transfer the meat to a platter. Discard the cloves, cinnamon stick, and orange peels. Add the dissolved cornstarch mixture to the pot. Stir until thick. Serve the meat with the sauce.

CHAPTER 6

POWER PRESSURE COOKER XL SEAFOOD RECIPES

Calamari in Tomato Sauce

Prep time: 15 min
Cook time: 30 min
Servings: 4

Ingredients

- 1 1/2 pounds of fresh or frozen calamari (thawed and drained)
- 1 bunch of parsley (chopped)
- 1 14.5-ounce can of chopped tomatoes
- A pinch of red pepper flakes
- 1/2 cup of white wine
- Salt and pepper to taste
- 1 garlic clove (smashed)
- Juice of 1 lemon
- Olive oil
- 2 anchovies

Directions

1. Make sure that the calamari is clean. Carefully remove the head from the hat. Be gentle in the process in order to get most of the innards in the head. Place it under running water as you pull the loose flesh off the hat.

   Let the water get through the hat in order to remove anything in there that needs to be cleaned. Tug and gently pull out the cartilage quill that feels like a stiff plastic. Slice the hat into strips and set aside.

Remove the tentacles from the eyes. Grab the middle beak of the tentacles and slowly squeeze its sides to pop. It is important that you clean all the calamari before cooking.

2. Press the **CHICKEN/MEAT** button of your pressure cooker. Wait for the pot to heat up. Put in the anchovies, garlic clove, 2 tablespoons of olive oil and a pinch of hot pepper. Saute for 3 minutes. Put in the calamari and saute for 5 minutes.
    Pour in the wine. Leave it for 3 minutes. Add half of the parsley. Pour in the contents of a can of chopped tomatoes. Fill the can with water, shake a bit, and add it to the cooker. Stir the ingredients until well combined.

3. Press the **KEEP WARM/CANCEL** button to reset the timer. Press the **MEAT/CHICKEN** button. Lock the lid in place and set the valve to pressure position. Once it is done, the pressure cooker will automatically go to keep warm mode. Turn the valve to the steam position to release pressure.

4. Open the lid. Add a bit of extra virgin olive oil and lemon juice, and stir. Transfer to a bowl and top with fresh parsley.

Mussels with Beer and Sausage

Prep time: 5 min
Cook time: 2 min
Servings: 4

Ingredients

- 2 pounds of mussels (cleaned and debearded)
- 8 ounces of sausage (spicy)
- 12 ounces of beer (bottle amber)
- 1 tablespoon each of mild paprika and olive oil
- 1 yellow onion (peeled and chopped)

Directions:

1. Press the **CHICKEN/MEAT** button of your pressure cooker. Wait for the pot to heat up. Heat oil and add the onion. Saute for 2 minutes.

   Stir in the sausages and cook until all sides are browned. Add the paprika and cook for 30 seconds. Put in the beer and mussels. Mix everything until combined.

2. Press the **KEEP WARM/CANCEL** button to reset the timer. Press the **FISH/VEGETABLES STEAM** button. Lock the lid in place and set the valve to pressure position. Once it is done, the cooker will automatically go to keep warm mode.

3. Turn the valve to the steam position to release pressure. Open the lid. Stir the ingredients and transfer the dish into serving bowls. Discard the mussels that did not open.

Shrimp Scampi Paella

Prep time: 2 min
Cook time: 5 min
Servings: 4

Ingredients

- 1 pound of wild-caught shrimp (frozen)
- Juice of 1 medium lemon
- 1 1/2 cups of filtered water
- 1 cup of Jasmine rice
- 1 teaspoon of sea salt
- Crushed red pepper to taste
- 4 garlic cloves (pressed)
- A pinch of saffron
- 1/4 teaspoon of black pepper
- 1/4 cup each of fresh parsley (chopped) and butter

Directions

1. Press the **BEANS/LENTILS** button. Put all the ingredients in the pressure cooker pot. Arrange the shrimp on top. Lock the lid in place and set the valve to pressure position. Once it is done, the cooker will automatically go to keep warm mode. Turn the valve to the steam position to release pressure.
2. You can serve the dish as is. You can also opt to peel the shells of the shrimps. Simply remove the shells and arrange the shrimps back onto the rice. Transfer to serving bowls and garnish with a squeeze of lemon juice, grated cheese, parsley, and butter.

Chickpeas with Shrimp and Cuttlefish

Prep time: 10 min
Cook time: 50 min
Servings: 4

Ingredients

- 1/2 pound of chickpeas (soaked in water overnight)
- 1 carrot
- 1 leek
- 1 bay leaf
- Salt to taste
- 1 pound of shrimp, plus shrimp heads
- 1 cuttlefish (chopped)
- 2 chili pepper
- 1 onion (chopped)
- Peppercorns

Directions

1. Put the shrimp heads in a saucepan, cover with water and cook for an hour. Strain the liquid and set it aside.
2. Press the **CHICKEN/MEAT** button of the pressure cooker. Set the timer to 20 minutes. Put the soaked chickpeas in the pot. Add water that is enough to cover the chickpeas. Lock the lid in place and set the valve to pressure position.

   Once it is done, the cooker will automatically go to keep warm mode. Turn the valve to the steam position to release pressure.

3. Heat oil in a saucepan over medium-high heat. Put in the onion and saute for 3 minutes. Stir in the shrimp, cuttlefish, and chili pepper. Add the cooked chickpeas. Pour enough shrimp broth to cover all the ingredients. Bring to a boil. Turn the heat to low and continue cooking for 20 minutes.

Octopus and Potatoes

Prep time: 20 min
Cook time: 35 min
Servings: 6

Ingredients

- 2 pounds each of potatoes and octopus
- Salt and pepper to taste
- Chopped parsley
- 3 garlic cloves
- 1/2 cup of olive oil
- 1 bay leaf
- 5 tablespoons of vinegar
- 1/2 teaspoon of peppercorns

Directions

1. Clean the octopus by removing the head. Cut its body in the middle. Discard the eyes and everything inside its body. Remove the beak in the area where the tentacles meet. Wash the octopus under running water until all the parts are clean.
2. Rinse the potatoes and scrub to clean thoroughly. Place them inside the pot of the pressure cooker. Press the **CHICKEN/MEAT** button to set the timer to 15 minutes.

   Add enough water to cover the mid mark of the potatoes and sprinkle with salt. Lock the lid in place and set the valve to pressure position.
3. Once it is done, the cooker will automatically go to keep warm mode. Turn the valve to the steam position to release pressure. Open the lid. Use tongs in removing the potatoes. Keep the cooking liquid.
4. Peel the potatoes while they are still hot. Hold them with a tong and use a fork in removing the skin.
5. Add more water to the pressure cooker. Put in some salt, 1 garlic clove, pepper, and bay leaf. Add the octopus, starting with the tentacles, once it boils.

Press the **KEEP WARM/CANCEL** button to reset the timer. Press the **CHICKEN/MEAT** button and continuously press the **TIME ADJUSTMENT** button until the cook time is set at 20 minutes. Lock the lid in place and set the valve to pressure position. Once it is done, turn the valve to the steam position to release pressure.

6. Strain the liquid. Cut the octopus into smaller chunks. Set aside. Chop the cooled potatoes with the size similar to the octopus.
7. Prepare the vinaigrette. Put the vinegar and olive oil in a small jar. Add salt and pepper, and 2 garlic cloves. Close the lid and shake the jar.
8. Put the chopped octopus and potatoes in a bowl. Pour in some of the vinaigrette. Toss to combine. Cover the bowl and chill. Top with parsley before serving.

Cod with Peas

Prep time: 20 min
Cook time: 5 min
Servings: 4

Ingredients

- 1/2 pound of frozen peas
- 1 pound of frozen cod fillet (thawed)
- 1 cup of wine
- 1/4 pound of parsley sprigs
- 1/2 teaspoon each of paprika and dry oregano
- 2 garlic cloves (halved)

Directions

1. Put the oregano, paprika, parsley sprigs, and garlic cloves into a food processor. Process a bit until chopped. Transfer the herb mixture to a bowl and mix it with wine.
2. Put the steamer basket inside the pressure cooker. Divide the fish into 4 and put them inside the basket. Press the **FISH/VEGETABLES STEAM** button. Lock the lid in place and set the valve to pressure position.
3. Once it is done, the cooker will automatically go to keep warm mode. Turn the valve to the steam position to release pressure. Open the lid. Transfer the fish to a platter. Remove the basket, but keep the pot inside.
4. Put the peas in the pot. Press the **KEEP WARM/CANCEL** button to reset the timer. Press the **FISH/VEGETABLES STEAM** button. Lock the lid in place and set the valve to pressure position. Once it is done, turn the valve to the steam position to release pressure.
5. Transfer the peas to a platter. Put the fish on top and drizzle with the herb mixture.

Mediterranean Style Fish

Prep time: 5 min
Cook time: 10 min
Servings: 4

Ingredients

- 1 pound of cherry tomatoes (halved)
- 4 white fish fillets
- 2 tablespoons of pickled capers
- 1 garlic clove (pressed)
- 1 cup of Taggiasche olives
- Salt and pepper to taste
- Thyme
- Olive oil

Directions

1. Put the cherry tomatoes on a heat-proof bowl. Cover them with thyme. Put the fish on top. Season with salt. Add oil and crushed garlic. Place the bowl inside the cooker. Press the **BEANS/LENTILS** button. Lock the lid in place and set the valve to pressure position.
2. Once it is done, the cooker will automatically go to keep warm mode. Turn the valve to the steam position to release pressure. Open the lid.
3. Transfer to plates. Top with herbs and more cherry tomatoes before serving.

Steamed Fish Fillet

Prep time: 10 min
Cook time: 10 min
Servings: 4

Ingredients

- 1 cup of olives
- 4 white fish fillets
- Olive oil
- 1 garlic clove (crushed)
- 1 pound of cherry tomatoes (sliced)
- Salt and pepper to taste
- A pinch of fresh thyme

Directions

1. Press the **SOUP/STEW** button of the pressure cooker. Pour a cup of water in the pot. Put the steamer basket inside. Arrange the fish fillet on top of the basket in a single layer. Put the olives and tomatoes on top of the fish. Sprinkle some salt and add a dash of olive oil. Put in some sprigs of fresh thyme and crushed garlic.
2. Lock the lid in place and set the valve to pressure position. Once it is done, the cooker will automatically go to keep warm mode. Turn the valve to the steam position to release pressure. Open the lid.
3. Transfer the fish to a platter. Sprinkle with a bit of olive oil, pepper, and thyme before serving.

Salmon Al Cartoccio

Prep time: 20 min
Cook time: 15 min
Servings: 4

Ingredients

- 3 potatoes (sliced)
- 4 salmon fillets
- 4 sprigs each of thyme and parsley
- 1 white onion (grated)
- Salt and pepper to taste
- Olive oil
- 1 lemon (sliced)

Directions

1. Divide the ingredients into 4 in order to make 4 pieces of the dish. Make each piece by following this order: Lay a parchment paper on a flat surface. Swirl some oil on it. Arrange the sliced potatoes in a single layer. Add more oil and season with salt and pepper. Put the fish fillet on top. Season with salt and pepper and drizzle with a little amount of oil.

   Add the onion rings, herbs, salt, lemon slices and a bit of oil. Fold the parchment paper. Cover it with a tin foil.

2. Press the **CHICKEN/MEAT** button of your pressure cooker. Pour 2 cups of water to the pot. Place the steamer basket inside. Put 2 fillets on top of the basket for each batch. Lock the lid in place and set the valve to pressure position.

3. Once it is done, turn the valve to the steam position to release pressure. Do not open the lid for 5 more minutes after all the pressure has come down. Do the same steps for the remaining packets of fish.

Coconut Fish Curry

Prep time: 5 min
Cook time: 15 min
Servings: 6-8

Ingredients

- 1 1/2 pounds of fish fillet (rinsed, sliced into bite-size pieces)
- 6 curry leaves
- 2 garlic cloves (pressed)
- 1 tomato (chopped)
- 1 tablespoon each of ground coriander and freshly grated ginger
- Salt to taste
- 2 cups of coconut milk (unsweetened)
- 2 onions (sliced into strips)
- 2 capsicums (sliced into strips)
- 1/2 teaspoon each of ground fenugreek and ground turmeric
- Lemon juice
- 1 teaspoon of hot pepper flakes
- 2 teaspoons of ground cumin

Directions

1. Press the **CHICKEN/MEAT** button of your pressure cooker. Wait for the pot to heat up. Add oil. Put in the curry leaves and cook for a minute. Add the ginger, garlic, and onion. Saute for 4 minutes.

   Stir in the 5 ground spices – fenugreek, turmeric, hot pepper, coriander, and cumin. Cook for a couple of minutes.

2. Deglaze by pouring in the coconut milk. Stir through the bottom of the pot. Put in the fish, tomatoes, and capsicum. Gently stir until the fish is covered with the mixture. Press the **KEEP WARM/CANCEL** button to reset the timer. Press the **BEANS/LENTILS** button.

   Lock the lid in place and set the valve to pressure position. Once it is done, turn the valve to the steam position to release pressure.

3. Open the lid. Season with salt and a bit of lemon juice before serving.

CHAPTER 7

POWER PRESSURE COOKER XL SOUPS AND STEWS RECIPES

Potato Cheese Soup

Prep time: 10 min
Cook time: 20 min
Servings: 6

Ingredients

- 2 14-ounce cans of chicken broth
- 6 cups of peeled potatoes (cut into cubes)
- 6 bacon slices (cooked and crumbled)
- 3 ounces of cream cheese (cubed)
- 2 tablespoons of cornstarch dissolved in 2 tablespoons of water
- 1 cup each of shredded cheddar cheese and frozen corn
- 1 teaspoon of salt
- 1/2 teaspoon of black pepper
- 2 tablespoons of dried parsley
- 1/8 teaspoon of red pepper flakes
- 1/2 cup of chopped onion
- 2 tablespoons of butter
- 2 cups of half and half

Directions

1. Press the **CHICKEN/MEAT** button of your pressure cooker. Wait for the pot to heat up. Melt the butter. Add the onions and saute for 5 minutes. Add the broth, red pepper flakes, parsley, salt, and pepper.

2. Put the steamer basket inside the pot. Place the potatoes in the basket. Press the **KEEP WARM/CANCEL** button to reset the timer. Press the **FISH/VEGETABLES STEAM** button and set the cook time to 4 minutes. Lock the lid in place and set the valve to pressure position. Once it is done, turn the valve to the steam position to release pressure.

3. Open the lid. Remove the steamer basket with the potatoes. Stir in the dissolved cornstarch into the pot. Add cream cheese and shredded cheese. Put in the rest of the ingredients. Simmer for 10 minutes but do not bring to a boil until done. Serve into individual bowls.

Creamy Mushroom Soup with Wine

Prep time: 5 min
Cook time: 15 min
Servings: 8

Ingredients

- 1 pound of baby portobello mushrooms (chopped)
- 4 cups of chicken stock
- 2 garlic cloves (chopped)
- 1/2 cup of dry Marsala wine
- 1 cup of onion (diced)
- 1/8 teaspoon of ground black pepper
- 1 teaspoon of salt
- 2 teaspoons each of fresh rosemary (chopped) and fresh thyme (chopped)
- 2 tablespoons of flour
- 4 tablespoons of butter (divided)
- 2 cups of heavy whipping cream
- Grated Parmesan cheese for garnish

Directions

1. Press the **CHICKEN/MEAT** button of your pressure cooker. Melt 2 tablespoons of butter once the pot heats up. Put in the onions and saute for 2 minutes. Add pepper, salt, mushrooms, and garlic. Cook for a couple of minutes.

   Add the wine. Cook for 2 minutes. Put in the rosemary, thyme and stock.

2. Press the **KEEP WARM/CANCEL** button to reset the timer. Press the **FISH/VEGETABLES STEAM** button and set the timer to 3 minutes. Lock the lid in place and set the valve to pressure position.
3. Melt the rest of the butter in a saucepan over medium heat. Stir as you add in the flour. Mix well and cook for 1 minute. Turn off the heat.

4. Once the timer of the pressure cooker is done, it will automatically go to keep warm mode. Turn the valve to the steam position to release pressure.

    Open the lid. Stir the mixture and bring it to a boil. Put in the flour and butter mixture. Simmer for 2 minutes. Use an immersion blender to process the soup until smooth. Stir in the cream.

5. Add grated Parmesan cheese on top of the soup before serving.

Rice and Vegetable Beef Soup

Prep time: 10 min
Cook time: 15 min
Servings: 6

Ingredients

- 1 pound of lean ground beef
- 1 14-ounce can of crushed tomatoes
- 2 14-ounce cans of beef broth
- 1 15-ounce can garbanzo beans (drained and rinsed)
- 1 potato (peeled and diced)
- 1 12-ounce bottle of Original V8 juice
- 1 onion (diced)
- 2 carrots (peeled and sliced)
- Salt and pepper to taste
- 1 rib celery (chopped)
- 3 cloves of garlic (chopped)
- 1 tablespoon of oil
- 1/2 cup each of long grain white rice and frozen peas (thawed)

Directions

1. Press the **CHICKEN/MEAT** button of your pressure cooker. Once the pot heats up, put in the meat and cook until all sides are browned. Transfer to a plate with paper towels to remove excess drippings.

    Add oil to the pot. Put in the onion and celery. Saute for 5 minutes. Put in the garlic and cook for 1 minute. Add the beef broth, V8 juice, beans, carrots, potatoes, and tomatoes. Put the browned meat back into the pot.

2. Press the **KEEP WARM/CANCEL** button to reset the timer. Press the **FISH/VEGETABLES STEAM** button and set the timer to 4 minutes. Lock the lid in place and set the valve to pressure position. Turn the valve to the steam position to release pressure once the timer is done.

3. Open the lid. Stir in the peas. Season with salt and pepper, if desired.

Turkey Noodle Soup

Prep time: 10 min
Cook time: 18 min
Servings: 6

Ingredients

- 6 cups of turkey stock
- 2 cups of turkey (diced)
- 1 onion (diced)
- 1 tablespoon of butter
- 4 carrots (peeled and sliced)
- Ground pepper
- 1 celery rib (diced)
- 1 teaspoon of salt
- Egg noodles (cooked)

Directions

1. Press the **CHICKEN/MEAT** button of your pressure cooker. Melt the butter once the pot heats up. Put in the onion and saute for 2 minutes. Add the carrots and celery. Saute for 5 more minutes. Add the meat and stock.
2. Press the **KEEP WARM/CANCEL** button to reset the timer. Press the **BEANS/LENTILS** button. Lock the lid in place and set the valve to pressure position. Once it is done, turn the valve to the steam position to release pressure.
3. Put the cooked noodles in a bowl. Pour the soup over the noodles and serve.

Garden Minestrone Soup

Prep time: 10 min
Cook time: 20 min
Servings: 6

Ingredients

- 1 14.5-ounce can of kidney beans
- 1 small zucchini (chopped)
- 3 pounds of tomatoes (peeled, seeded and minced)
- 2 carrots (diced)
- 2 14.5-ounce cans of chicken broth
- 2 tablespoons of fresh basil (chopped)
- 1 teaspoon of Italian seasoning
- 1 celery stalk (diced)
- 1 onion (chopped)
- 4 cloves garlic (minced)
- 1 cup of fresh corn kernels
- 1 tablespoon of olive oil
- 2 cups of baby spinach
- 1 cup each of grated Asiago cheese and ditalini pasta (uncooked)
- 1 teaspoon of salt
- 1/2 teaspoon of ground black pepper

Directions

1. Press the **CHICKEN/MEAT** button of your pressure cooker. Put in the oil once the pot heats up. Add the onion and saute for 5 minutes.

   Put in the veggies and cook for 5 minutes while you stir. Add the broth, tomatoes, and seasoning. Season with salt.

2. Press the **KEEP WARM/CANCEL** button to reset the timer. Press the **FISH/VEGETABLES STEAM** button and set the timer to 4 minutes. Lock the lid in place and set the valve to pressure position. Turn the valve to the steam position to release pressure once the timer is done. Add the spinach, beans, and basil to the soup and stir.

3. Sprinkle cheese on top before serving.

Poblano Corn Chowder

Prep time: 10 min
Cook time: 20 min
Servings: 8

Ingredients

- 4 cups of potatoes (peeled and cut into cubes)
- 2 celery stalks (peeled and diced)
- 2 garlic cloves (minced)
- 1 onion (diced)
- 1 large poblano pepper (with the ribs and seeds removed/diced)
- 2 14-ounce cans of chicken broth
- 1 tablespoon of olive oil
- 2 large carrots (peeled and diced)
- 2 cups of half and half
- 1 teaspoon of salt
- 1/2 teaspoon each of dried thyme and black pepper
- 3 tablespoons of cornstarch dissolved in 3 tablespoons of water
- A dash of red pepper flakes
- 4 cups of frozen corn

Directions

1. Press the **CHICKEN/MEAT** button of your pressure cooker. Put in oil once the pot heats up. Add the onion, celery, and carrots. Saute for 5 minutes.

   Put in the poblano pepper and garlic. Saute for a minute. Add 1 can of broth, red pepper flakes, thyme, and parsley. Season with salt and pepper. Put the steamer basket inside the pot and place the potatoes in the basket.

2. Press the **KEEP WARM/CANCEL** button to reset the timer. Press the **FISH/VEGETABLES STEAM** button and set the timer to 4 minutes. Lock the lid in place and set the valve to pressure position. Once it is done, turn the valve to the steam position to release pressure.

3. Open the lid. Remove the basket and potatoes. Simmer the soup. Stir in the dissolved cornstarch mixture. Once the soup thickens, add the rest of the broth, corn, half and half, and put the potatoes back into the pot.

Black Bean Stew with Picante Chicken

Prep time: 10 min
Cook time: 20 min
Servings: 10

Ingredients

- 3 1/2 cups of chicken broth
- 2 chicken breasts (skinless)
- 1 10-ounce can of tomatoes with green chilies
- 3 cups organic canned or cooked black beans
- 1 tablespoon of dried cilantro
- 1 4-ounce can of diced green chilies
- 1 teaspoon each ancho chili powder, onion powder, ground cumin, and garlic powder
- 1/4 teaspoon of oregano

Directions

1. Put in 1 cup of beans and 1 cup of broth in a blender. Process until pureed.

   Put the mixture in the pressure cooker pot. Add the meat, spices, tomatoes and the remaining broth. Press the **RICE/RISOTTO** button and set the timer to 8 minutes. Lock the lid in place and set the valve to pressure position. Once it is done, turn the valve to the steam position to release pressure.

2. Open the lid. Transfer the meat to a plate and shred it using 2 forks. Put the shredded chicken breasts back into the pot. Add the remaining beans and fresh scallions. Simmer the soup for a couple of minutes.

Ratatouille Vegetable Stew

Prep time: 3 min
Cook time: 7 min
Servings: 6

Ingredients

- 2 zucchinis (sliced)
- 1 eggplant (peeled and cut into cubes)
- 2 tomatoes (chopped)
- 4 tablespoons of canola oil
- 1/4 cup of chicken or vegetable stock
- 2 green peppers (seeded and cut into strips)
- 2 tablespoons of parsley (minced)
- 2 garlic cloves (minced)
- 1 onion (chopped)
- 1 potato (diced)

Directions

1. Press the **CHICKEN/MEAT** button of your pressure cooker. Wait for the pot to heat up before adding half of the oil. Put in the peppers, zucchini, eggplant, and potato. Stir fry for 2 minutes and transfer to a plate.

   Add the remaining oil into the pot. Put in the onion and garlic, and saute for 3 minutes. Put the vegetables back to the pot.

2. Press the **KEEP WARM/CANCEL** button to reset the timer. Press the **FISH/VEGETABLES STEAM** button and set the timer to 4 minutes. Lock the lid in place and set the valve to pressure position.

   Once it is done, turn the valve to the steam position to release pressure. Open the lid. Simmer the soup for 2 minutes.

Potato and Green Bean Casserole

Prep time: 2 min
Cook time: 3 min
Servings: 4-6

Ingredients

- 1/2 pound of green beans
- 3 potatoes (peeled and cut into small cubes)
- 1/2 cup of chicken stock
- 1 green pepper (diced)
- 1 medium onion (minced)
- 1 garlic clove (minced)
- 1 tablespoon each of olive oil and parsley (minced)
- Salt and pepper to taste

Directions

1. Put all the ingredients in the pressure cooker pot. Press the **FISH/VEGETABLES STEAM** button and set the timer to 3 minutes. Lock the lid in place and set the valve to pressure position.
2. Once it is done, the cooker will automatically go to keep warm mode. Turn the valve to the steam position to release pressure.

Chickpea and Spinach Soup

Prep time: 5 min
Cook time: 14 min
Servings: 6

Ingredients

- 2 cups of dried chickpeas (soaked for 4 hours, rinsed and drained)
- Vegetable stock or water
- 2 potatoes (quartered)
- 1/4 cup of canola oil
- 8 ounces of spinach
- Salt and pepper to taste
- 3 garlic cloves
- 2 onions (quartered)

Directions

1. Put the soaked chickpeas into the pressure cooker pot. Add the stock, garlic cloves, potatoes, and onions. Press the **SOUP/STEW** button and set the timer to 14 minutes. Lock the lid in place and set the valve to pressure position. Turn the valve to the steam position to release pressure once the timer is done. Scoop out 1 1/2 cups of the cooked chickpeas and set them aside.
2. Puree the soup in the pot by using an immersion blender. Add more liquid, if preferred. Stir in the spinach and oil.
3. Press the **KEEP WARM/CANCEL** button to reset the timer. Press the **FISH/VEGETABLES STEAM** button. Lock the lid in place and set the valve to pressure position. Once it is done, the cooker will automatically go to keep warm mode. Turn the valve to the steam position to release pressure. Open the lid and stir in the reserved chickpeas.

CHAPTER 8

POWER PRESSURE COOKER XL VEGAN RECIPES

Red Cabbage Salad

Prep time: 5 min
Cook time: 3 min
Servings: 4

Ingredients

- 2 teaspoons of red wine vinegar
- 1/4 cup of onion (thinly sliced)
- 2 cups of red cabbage (shredded)
- Salt and pepper to taste
- 1/2 teaspoon of brown sugar
- 1 tablespoon of canola oil

Directions

1. Put the steamer basket inside the pot of the pressure cooker. Put the cabbage in the basket. Press the **FISH/VEGETABLES STEAM** button and set the timer to 3 minutes. Lock the lid in place and set the valve to pressure position.

   Once it is done, turn the valve to the steam position to release pressure.

2. Remove the basket. Rinse the cooked cabbage with cold water to stop it from cooking. Place the cooked cabbage in a bowl. Add the rest of the ingredients and toss to combine.

Crumb-Topped Vegetables

Prep time: 3 min
Cook time: 3 min
Servings: 4

Ingredients

- 1 teaspoon of lemon juice
- 1 pound of carrots (peeled and cut into sticks)
- 1/4 cup of dry bread crumbs
- 3 tablespoons of butter
- 1 tablespoon of minced parsley

Directions

1. Press the **CHICKEN/MEAT** button of your pressure cooker. Melt the butter once the pot heats up. Add the bread crumbs and cook until crunchy. Put in the lemon juice and parsley, and stir. Transfer the mixture to a bowl.
2. Wipe the pot with paper towels. Add 1- 3/4 cups of water. Put the steamer basket inside. Place the carrots in the basket. Season with salt and pepper. Press the **KEEP WARM/CANCEL** button to reset the timer. Press the **FISH/VEGETABLES STEAM** button and set the timer to 3 minutes. Lock the lid in place and set the valve to pressure position. Turn the valve to the steam position to release pressure once the timer is done.
3. Open the lid. Remove the basket and drain the liquid. Put the carrots on a plate. Top with the crumb mixture and serve.

Candied Yams

Prep time: 5 min
Cook time: 8 min
Servings: 4

Ingredients

- 2 pieces of sweet potatoes (peeled, cut in half lengthwise)
- 1 teaspoon of grated orange zest
- 1/32 teaspoon (or 1 scoop) of stevia extract
- 1 cup of orange juice
- 2 tablespoons of butter
- Salt to taste

Directions

1. Put the orange juice in the pressure cooker pot. Place the steamer basket inside and put the potato slices in it. Season with stevia extract, salt, and orange zest. Lightly brush the potatoes with butter.

   Press the **RICE/RISOTTO** button and set the timer to 8 minutes. Lock the lid in place and set the valve to pressure position.

   Once it is done, turn the valve to the steam position to release pressure. Open the lid and transfer the potatoes to a plate.

2. Simmer sauce in the pot while constantly stirring. Turn off the cooker once the sauce becomes thick. Pour it over the sweet potatoes and serve.

Indian Curry

Prep time: 10 min
Cook time: 20 min
Servings: 4

Ingredients

- 1 eggplant (cubed)
- 1 small squash (cubed)
- 5-ounce can of evaporated milk (fat-free)
- 1 cup each of pressure-cooked chickpeas and quinoa
- 1/3 teaspoon each of garam masala and curry powder
- A pinch of saffron threads (soaked in 2 cups of warm water)
- 1/2 cup each of green beans and onions (diced)
- 2 cups of warm water
- 2/3 teaspoon of hot Madras curry powder
- 1 sweet potato (cubed)
- 1 tablespoon of butter
- 1 teaspoon each of cumin seeds and coconut extract
- Half of a hot pepper (sliced)

Directions

1. Put the saffron with water in the bottom of the pressure cooker pan. Add the quinoa, chickpeas, and coconut extract. Place the trivet inside. Put the squash and sweet potato on the steamer basket. Add the pepper, eggplant, and beans.

   Place the basket on top of the trivet. Press the **RICE/RISOTTO** button and set the timer to 8 minutes. Lock the lid in place and set the valve to pressure position.

2. Melt butter in a pan over low flame. Add the cumin seeds and cook for 2 minutes. Add the onions and saute for a couple of minutes. Stir in the rest of the spices and add milk. Simmer for 10 minutes.

3. Once the pressure cooker is done, it will automatically go to keep warm mode. Turn the valve to the steam position to release pressure. Open the lid and put the cooked vegetables into a bowl. Add the curry sauce and toss to combine.

4. Fluff the quinoa at the pot's bottom. Simmer it longer if you find it too watery. Ladle into serving bowls and add curry on top.

Potato Leek Pea Soup

Prep time: 5 min
Cook time: 12 min
Servings: 4-6

Ingredients

- 1 pound of potatoes (cubed)
- 4 leeks (rinsed, drained and finely chopped)
- 4 cups of vegetable stock
- 1 cup each of peas and milk
- 1 onion (finely chopped)
- 2 tablespoons each of parsley (minced) and canola oil
- Salt and pepper to taste

Directions

1. Press the **CHICKEN/MEAT** button of your pressure cooker. Heat the oil. Cook the leeks and onion until soft. Stir in the parsley, peas, and potatoes. Pour in the milk and stock. Season with salt and pepper.
2. Press the **KEEP WARM/CANCEL** button to reset the timer. Press the **SOUP/STEW** button and set the timer to 12 minutes. Lock the lid in place and set the valve to pressure position. Turn the valve to the steam position to release pressure once the timer is done.
3. Cool the soup a bit. Use an immersion blender to puree the soup until soft. Top the soup with croutons before serving.

Diced Potato and Pea Curry

Prep time: 5 min
Cook time: 12 min
Servings: 4-6

Ingredients

- 1 cup of frozen peas
- 6 potatoes (peeled and cut into small pieces)
- 1 teaspoon each of cumin powder, cumin seeds, ginger paste, garam masala, dry mango powder, garlic paste, and red chili powder
- 2 teaspoons of coriander powder
- 1 onion (diced)
- 1/2 teaspoon of turmeric powder
- 2 tomatoes (diced)
- 2 green chilies (slit)
- 1/2 cup of water
- 2 tablespoons each of canola oil and of fresh coriander (finely chopped)
- Salt to taste

Directions

1. Press the **CHICKEN/MEAT** button of your pressure cooker. Heat the oil and saute the cumin seeds for 1 minute. Stir in the green chilies, add the onion, and cook for 4 minutes. Add the ginger and garlic paste. Stir the ingredients for 1 minute.

   Add the rest of the seasonings except for the garam masala. Stir in the ingredients along with the tomatoes. Add the potatoes, peas, and water. Press the **KEEP WARM/CANCEL** button to reset the timer. Press the **RICE/RISOTTO** button and set the timer to 8 minutes.

2. Once the timer is done, turn the valve to the steam position to release pressure. Open the lid. Transfer to a bowl and sprinkle garam masala on top. Cover and let it rest for 2 minutes. Top the dish with coriander leaves before serving.

Stir-Fried Broccoli

Prep time: 3 min
Cook time: 3 min
Servings: 4-6

Ingredients

- 1 bunch of broccoli (trim the stems, cut into florets)
- 6 tablespoons of vegetable stock
- Salt to taste
- 2 tablespoons each of soy sauce and sesame oil
- 1 small slice of fresh ginger
- 1 garlic clove (crushed and peeled)

Directions

1. Press the **CHICKEN/MEAT** button of your pressure cooker. Heat oil in the pot. Cook the ginger and garlic for 2 minutes. Add the broccoli and fry for 3 minutes. Sprinkle a bit of salt.

   Put the stir-fried broccoli into the steamer basket. Put the stock and soy sauce into the pot. Place the basket with the broccoli inside.

2. Press the **KEEP WARM/CANCEL** button to reset the timer. Press the **FISH/VEGETABLES STEAM** button and set the timer to 3 minutes. Lock the lid in place and set the valve to pressure position. Once it is done, turn the valve to the steam position to release pressure.

3. Open the lid. Remove the steamer basket and put the veggies on a platter. Drizzle with some of the cooking liquid before serving.

German Potato Salad

Prep time: 10 min
Cook time: 3 min
Servings: 4

Ingredients

- 4 bacon slices
- 4 potatoes (thinly sliced)
- 3 tablespoons of vinegar
- 1 onion (thinly sliced)
- 1 teaspoon of mustard
- Salt and pepper
- 1/2 teaspoon of celery seed
- 1/2 scoop of stevia extract

Directions

1. Press the **CHICKEN/MEAT** button of your pressure cooker. Fry the bacon slices until crisp. Transfer to a plate with paper towels to absorb excess dripping. Crumble the bacon to bits.
2. Keep 1 tablespoon of the bacon dripping. Clean the pot by wiping it with paper towels. Transfer the dripping to a bowl. Add vinegar, sugar, and mustard. Mix well.
3. Add 1-3/4 cups of water to the pressure cooker pot. Place the steamer basket inside. Arrange the potatoes and onions in layers in the basket. Season with salt and pepper. Add celery seeds and the crumbled bacon. Drizzle with the vinegar and mustard mixture. Press the **KEEP WARM/CANCEL** button to reset the timer. Press the **FISH/VEGETABLES STEAM** button and set the timer to 3 minutes. Lock the lid in place and set the valve to pressure position.

   Turn the valve to the steam position to release pressure once the timer is done. Open the lid and serve the dish.

Country-Style Potatoes

Prep time: 3 min
Cook time: 7 min
Servings: 4

Ingredients

- 4 cups of potatoes (sliced into 1/2-inch thickness)
- 1/8 pound of fresh mushrooms (sliced and the stems trimmed)
- 1/2 cup of water or chicken stock
- 1 tablespoon of olive oil
- 2 tablespoons of parsley (minced)
- Salt and pepper
- 1/2 cup of finely chopped onion

Directions

1. Press the **CHICKEN/MEAT** button of your pressure cooker. Heat the oil. Cook the mushrooms and onion for 3 minutes. Add the remaining ingredients and stir for a couple of minutes.
2. Press the **KEEP WARM/CANCEL** button to reset the timer. Press the **FISH/VEGETABLES STEAM** button and set the timer to 4 minutes. Lock the lid in place and set the valve to pressure position. Once it is done, turn the valve to the steam position to release pressure.

Vegetable Mélange

Prep time: 3 min
Cook time: 6 min
Servings: 4

Ingredients

- 3 tomatoes (chunked and with the seeds removed)
- 4 potatoes (peeled and thinly sliced)
- 1/2 cup of canola oil
- 3 celery stalks (sliced)
- 2 zucchinis (cut into large chunks)
- 2 carrots (thinly sliced)
- 1 green pepper (seeds removed and sliced)
- 1 onion (chopped)
- 1 garlic clove (chopped)
- 2 cups of frozen peas (thawed)
- 1 cup of vegetable or chicken stock
- 3/4 cup of red split lentils
- 1 teaspoon of fresh basil (chopped)
- Salt and pepper
- 1/4 cup of fresh dill (diced) or a teaspoon of dried dill
- 1/4 cup of parsley (diced)

Directions

1. Press the **CHICKEN/MEAT** button of your pressure cooker. Heat oil and saute the parsley, dill, and garlic for 1 minute. Put in the red split lentils, veggies, and stock. Stir everything and season with salt and pepper.
2. Press the **KEEP WARM/CANCEL** button to reset the timer. Press the **RICE/RISOTTO** button. Lock the lid in place and set the valve to pressure position. Turn the valve to the steam position to release pressure once the timer is done.
3. Open the lid. Stir the veggies and drain the liquid. Transfer to cups and serve.

CHAPTER 9

POWER PRESSURE COOKER XL DESSERT RECIPES

Pumpkin Date Brown Rice Pudding

Prep time: 30 min
Cook time: 20 min
Servings: 6

Ingredients

- 1 stick of cinnamon
- 3 cups of dairy-free milk
- 1 cup each of pureed pumpkin and short grain brown rice
- 1/2 cup each of water and pitted dates (cut into small pieces)
- 1/4 cup of raw honey (mixed with 1 tablespoon of liquid)
- 1 teaspoon each of vanilla extract and pumpkin spice mix
- 1/8 teaspoon of salt

Directions

1. Put the rice in a bowl. Pour boiling water and soak for an hour. Rinse.
2. Put the milk and boiling water in the pressure cooker pot. Add the soaked rice, cinnamon stick, and salt. Press the **MEAT/CHICKEN** button and set the timer to 20 minutes. Lock the lid in place and set the valve to pressure position. Turn the valve to the steam position to release pressure once the timer is done.
3. Open the lid. Let the mixture simmer while you stir in the pumpkin puree, honey mixture, and pumpkin spice mix. Turn off the cooker. Add the vanilla and discard the cinnamon stick. Pour the dish into a bowl, cover and let it cool for 30 minutes.

Pressure Cooker Cheesecake

Prep time: 10 min
Cook time: 25 min
Servings: 6

Ingredients

For the crust
- 2 tablespoons of melted butter
- 1 cup of crushed cookie crumbs

For the filling
- 2 eggs
- 1 teaspoon of vanilla extract
- 16 ounces of cream cheese
- 1/32 teaspoon (or 1 scoop) of stevia extract
- 1/4 cup of sour cream
- 1 tablespoon of flour

Directions

1. Mix the butter and cookie crumbs. Press the mixture at the bottom of a springform pan. Put in the fridge for 10 minutes.
2. Combine the sugar and cream cheese in a bowl. Gradually add the eggs, sour cream, vanilla, and flour. Mix well. Transfer the mixture to the springform pan with the chilled crust.
3. Pour a cup of water in the pressure cooker pot. Place the trivet inside. Put the springform pan with the cheesecake mixture on top of the trivet. Press the **CHICKEN/MEAT** button and set the timer to 25 minutes. Lock the lid in place and set the valve to pressure position.

   Turn the valve to the steam position to release pressure once the timer is done.

4. Open the lid. Refrigerate the cheesecake for four hours after it has completely cooled down.

Pressure Cooker Applesauce

Prep time: 5 min
Cook time: 4 min
Servings: 6

Ingredients

- 1 teaspoon of ground cinnamon
- 1/4 cup of water
- 1/2 scoop of stevia extract
- 10 large apples (peeled, cored and sliced)

Directions

1. Put everything in the pressure cooker pot and stir. Press the **FISH/VEGETABLES STEAM** button and set the timer to 4 minutes. Lock the lid in place and set the valve to pressure position. Turn the valve to the steam position to release pressure once it is done.
2. Open the lid. Transfer the mixture to a food processor. Process until smooth.

Bread Pudding with Caramel Pecan Sauce

Prep time: 10 min
Cook time: 18 min
Servings: 6

Ingredients

For the sauce
- 2 tablespoons each of heavy cream and butter
- 1 teaspoon of vanilla extract
- 1/2 teaspoon of salt
- 1/2 cup of toasted and chopped pecans

For the pudding
- 3 eggs (beaten)
- 7 thick slices of cinnamon bread (cubed and toasted)
- 1/2 cup of raisins
- 3 cups whole milk
- 1/2 teaspoon of ground cinnamon
- 1 teaspoon of vanilla extract
- 4 tablespoons of melted butter
- 1/4 teaspoon of salt
- 1/32 teaspoon (or 1 scoop) of stevia extract

Directions

1. Whisk the eggs in a bowl. Add the vanilla, cinnamon, milk, butter, salt, and stevia extract. Put the bread and raisins in the mixture. Soak them for 20 minutes. Once soaked, transfer everything into a baking dish. Cover it with a foil.
2. Add 1-1/2 cups of water to the pressure cooker pot. Put the trivet inside and place the baking dish on top. Press the **CHICKEN/MEAT** button and set the timer to 18 minutes. Lock the lid in place and set the valve to pressure position.

   Once it is done, the cooker will automatically go to keep warm mode. Turn the valve to the steam position to release pressure.

3. Mix the ingredients for the sauce. In a saucepan over medium heat, combine the heavy cream and butter. Continue stirring as you bring it to a boil. Turn the heat to low. Add the vanilla and chopped pecans. Mix well.
4. Slice the bread pudding and drizzle with the sauce before serving.

Poached Pears with Chocolate Sauce

Prep time: 5 min
Cook time: 3 min
Servings: 6

Ingredients

- 3 cups of water
- 2 cups of white wine
- 2 scoops of stevia extract
- 6 pears (ripe and firm)
- 6 cinnamon sticks
- 1 lemon (divided in half)

For the sauce

- 1 tablespoon of raw honey (mixed with 1 teaspoon of liquid)
- 1/4 cup of coconut oil
- 1/2 cup of coconut milk
- 9 ounces bittersweet chocolate (cut into small pieces)

Directions

1. Press the **CHICKEN/MEAT** button of your pressure cooker. Wait for the pot to heat up before adding the wine and water. Stir in the stevia extract and cinnamon sticks. Bring to a boil.

2. Peel the fruits. Rub the flesh with lemon. Squeeze the rest of the lemon into the pot with the syrup. Place the pears into the pot. Press the **FISH/VEGETABLES STEAM** button. Set the timer to 3 minutes.

   Lock the lid in place and set the valve to pressure position. Turn the valve to the steam position to release pressure once the timer is done.

3. Open the lid. Transfer the pears to a bowl. Pour the syrup on top. Set aside to cool.

4. Stir in the honey mixture, coconut oil, and coconut milk in a saucepan over medium heat. Bring to a boil. Remove from heat.

5. Put the chopped bittersweet chocolates in a bowl. Pour in the hot mixture. Wait for a minute before stirring the chocolate sauce until smooth.
6. Cut the bottom of the pears. Drizzle them with the chocolate sauce before serving.

Raspberry Curd

Prep time: 3 min
Cook time: 6 min
Servings: 8

Ingredients

- 12 ounces of fresh raspberries
- 2 egg yolks
- 2 tablespoons each of fresh lemon juice and butter
- 4 scoops of stevia extract

Directions

1. Combine the raspberries, stevia extract, and lemon juice in the pressure cooker pot. Press the **FISH/VEGETABLES STEAM** button. Lock the lid in place and set the valve to pressure position. Turn the valve to the steam position to release pressure once the timer is done.
2. Open the lid. Puree the mixture in a processor. Strain and discard the seeds.
3. Press the **CHICKEN/MEAT** button of your pressure cooker. Combine the pureed raspberry and whisked egg yolks in the pot. Bring the mixture to a boil while stirring often. Stir in the butter until melted. Turn off the pressure cooker. Allow the mixture to cool a bit before transferring to a container. Refrigerate before serving.

Rice Pudding

Prep time: 3 min
Cook time: 6 min
Servings: 6

Ingredients

- 1 cup of Arborio rice
- 2 eggs
- 2 cups whole milk (divided)
- 1/2 teaspoon of vanilla extract
- 3/4 cup of raisins
- 1/32 teaspoon (or 1 scoop) of stevia extract
- 1 1/2 cups of water
- 1/4 teaspoon of salt

Directions

1. Put the rice, salt, and water in pressure cooker pot. Press the **FISH/VEGETABLES STEAM** button. Set the timer to 3 minutes. Lock the lid in place and set the valve to pressure position. Turn the valve to the steam position to release pressure once the timer is done.
2. Open the lid. Add half of the milk and stevia extract to the mixture. Stir until combined.
3. In a bowl, whisk the eggs, vanilla, and the rest of the milk. Strain the mixture and transfer it into the pot.
4. Press the **CHICKEN/MEAT** button of your pressure cooker. Bring the mixture to a boil while stirring often. Add the raisins and stir.

Hazelnut Flan

Prep time: 5 min
Cook time: 6 min
Servings: 8

Ingredients

- 3 whole eggs, plus 2 egg yolks
- 2 cups of whole milk
- 1/2 cup of whipping cream
- 2 tablespoons of hazelnut syrup
- A pinch of salt
- 1/32 teaspoon (or 1 scoop) of stevia extract
- 1 teaspoon of vanilla extract
- 1/4 cup of raw honey (mixed with 1 tablespoon of liquid)

Directions

1. Whisk the eggs, yolks, stevia extract, and salt in a bowl. Put the milk in a saucepan and heat over medium flame. Gradually mix the heated milk to the egg mixture. Add the vanilla, cream, and hazelnut syrup. Mix well. Strain the mixture and pour into 8 custard cups. Cover the cups with foil.
2. Put a cup of water in the pressure cooker. Put in the trivet and place the custard cups on top. Press the **FISH/VEGETABLES STEAM** button. Lock the lid in place and set the valve to pressure position. Turn the valve to the steam position to release pressure once the timer is done.
3. Open the lid. Cool the custard cups with the flan. Cover each with plastic and refrigerate. Drizzle with raw honey and top with whipped cream before serving.

Tapioca Pudding

Prep time: 3 min
Cook time: 6 min
Servings: 4

Ingredients

- 2 egg yolks
- 1/2 cup each of whole milk and small-pearl tapioca
- 1/32 teaspoon (or 1 scoop) of stevia extract
- 1/2 teaspoon of vanilla extract
- 1/4 teaspoon of salt
- 1 1/2 cups of water

Directions

1. Put the tapioca and water in the pressure cooker pot. Press the **RICE/RISOTTO** button. Lock the lid in place and set the valve to pressure position. Turn the valve to the steam position to release pressure once the timer is done.
2. Open the lid. Add the stevia extract and salt to the cooked tapioca. Whisk until combined.
3. In a bowl, whisk the egg yolks and mix. Strain and transfer the mixture into the pot. Press the **CHICKEN/MEAT** button of your pressure cooker and bring it to a boil. Turn off the pressure cooker. Add the vanilla and stir.

Pumpkin Crème Brûlée

Prep time: 5 min
Cook time: 6 min
Servings: 6

Ingredients

- 3 scoops of stevia extract
- 1/3 cup of granulated sugar
- 6 egg yolks
- 1/4 teaspoon of pumpkin pie spice
- 1 teaspoon of vanilla extract
- 1/2 teaspoon of cinnamon
- A pinch of salt
- 1/4 cup of pumpkin puree
- 2 cups of heavy cream

Directions

1. In a bowl, combine the pumpkin puree, stevia extract, vanilla, and egg yolks.
2. Put a saucepan over medium flame. Combine the heavy cream, pumpkin pie spice, cinnamon, and salt. Mix well and simmer. Remove from heat. Gradually combine this with the first mixture. Divide them into 2 ramekins and cover with foil.
3. Pour 1 cup of water into the pressure cooker pot. Place the trivet inside the pot. Put the ramekins on top. Press the **FISH/VEGETABLES STEAM** button. Lock the lid in place and set the valve to pressure position. Turn the valve to the steam position to release pressure once the timer is done.
4. Open the lid. Wait for the cups to cool before putting them in the fridge.

CONCLUSION

Thank you again for getting a copy of this book!

I hope this book was able to help you to master how to use the Power Pressure Cooker XL in coming up with different dishes that you can serve any time of the day.

Good luck!

Printed in Great Britain
by Amazon